There is only one way to find Him, and that's leaving Egypt behind and following God to the desolate desert in a surrendered position.

—"Hunger in the Desert," Desert Oasis '97

In the beginning was the Word, and the Word was with God, and the Word was God.

John 1:1

September 6, 1999.

I'm Really glad that the Labor Day holiday is over. Boy did I put away some "Unnecessary" food this week-end. I feel like I'm 10 month Pregnant, not to mention how I look. Well, tomorrow is a new day. I'll wake up (if the Good Lord is willing) and monitor my food intake again. Most of the foods that I'm eating are Breads, Sweets, Fried Food and Soda's again so what I will start tomorrow is to Cut out all of these items especially Sugar & Sweets. I also will need to exercise Cory will love that because he will get to Ride his bike while I walk. Now I will pray to God to bless me with the determination I will need. Help me Lord if you will.

When you hear the lie, quote the truth, and then focus on the will of God.

—"Stay Awake" audiotape

Love the LORD your God and keep his requirements, his decrees,
his laws and his commands always.

Deuteronomy 11:1

September 7, 1999   "307"

Today started off good. For breakfast
I ate 2 boiled Eggs which was
not bad. I had a Cup of decaf
Coffee. My hungry was gone Also
Lunch will be Tuna w/ Mayo. Sorry
Can opener at work did not work.
Will wait until I get home to eat.
Dranked 1 gal of water today Plus
A Cup of decaf tea. Dinner Consist
of String beans and Barbucue
Wingnetts (6).

September 8, 1999...

Today was good. God woke me up this
morning and got me going. For breakfast
I had 2 Boiled Eggs w/ 4 slices of bacon.
I didn't do the Salt but I did have Pepper
along w/ decaf Coffee w/ Squal. Lots of
Water also. For Lunch I had Tuna
Packed in Water and a cup of decaf
Tea w/ Equal. Dinner Consist of A Salad

And Chicken (Fried). I also had a box of Orange Juice. The last time I weighed at the Doctors office I came in @ 307. Today I weighed in @ 302. Cool——— Let's See what happens Tomorrow.

September 9, 1999.   "300"
God is Good. I'm feeling a little lighter. My Stomach looks like it went down a fraction. Shirley has really been encouraging me and that means Alot because it keeps me going. For breakfast we had 2 Boiled Eggs & Bacon (4). I also had Orange Juice and Coffee (It was Regular) I don't know how to make Coffee at work. Lunch included a Salad w/Ranch dressing and a Chicken breast (small) and 1 Wingette. Along w/ a cup of Green/mint Tea. I drank a Gallon of water and I also Walked while Cory Rode his bicycle. I even did a little stretching when I Returned.

Stop working on the obedience and start working on the love— the obedience will follow.
—"The Promised Land," Desert Oasis '97

David said about him: "'I saw the Lord always before me.
Because he is at my right hand, I will not be shaken.'"

Acts 2:25

September 10, 1999
Today, I started out with the 2 boiled
eggs & BAcon for breakfast. For lunch
I had A salad with Turkey breast lunch
meat and Tea (Ginsing)

I came home with the intention of washing
my cloths, hair and cleaning my Room.
Certain things made me compel to stay
in my Room, so I cleaned my Room
changed the bed, washed my hair and
took care of Cory.

September 11, 1999 (296) what a beautiful
day the Lord has blessed us to see.
I stayed in the house all day. I
washed my cloths, watched movies on
TV and played w/ Cory. For Breakfast
I had Samon cakes & boiled Eggs
w/Tea. I'm ironing Cory's cloths when
the Phone rings. Its "JACK." surprise

He wanted to know if I wanted to go to the movies. I met him in Greenbelt to se MARtin Lawrence's New movie. We left there and went to Dove Down and had dinner, and Played the slots some. We left for home about 1:30.

September 12, 1999
I missed the 7:30 service and the 10:00 service. "Very Bad" I had A chance to go to the game but Shirley went because She watched Cory for me when I went out with Jack.
I ate the wrong foods. I though the Potatoe Skins I had for dinner were OK but they werent. I had A Candy Bar, Ice Cream Sandwich and. Potatoes w/f Chicken wings for Sunday dinner A Sandwich w/ Corn chips. I Just went for it. I did go For A WAlK w/ Cory

Life is overwhelming if you don't know about this coordinated Genius that can take care of any need.
—"True Repentance" audiotape

> *"For I know the plans I have for you,"* declares the LORD, *"plans to prosper you and not to harm you, plans to give you hope and a future."*
>
> Jeremiah 29:11

September 13, 1999.
Breakfast 2 eggs w/3 Bacon - Tea
Not hungry @ lunch because I at @ 10:00
September 20, 1999   "287"
Well, I haven't written in my journal in a few
days. For the most part I have been under
control but there is also room for improvement.
Today I did start over again. I set a
goal of 5-6 lbs for this week. Yesterday
Angela, TaT, Shirley and I went to the
Lincoln Theater to see T.D Jakes play "Women
Thou Art Loose". It was very good.
Need to see more plays. The Job Training #3
really "Bad" for me. It's really stressing
me out. I continue to pray to God for
the understanding I need to pass this class.
September 21, 1999.
Well, let's see what today will bring. Not
looking forward to work. Well, I can say I
have my food under control today. I don't
feel to good about the foods I'm eating.

I feel that I need to eat more fruit & vegetables, and less Red meat. The office was terrible. I feel like I'm taking French or some foreign language. There are so many different places to get information. I understand to a degree but I don't seem to be Putting it together. I Really feel like quitting this Job (For Real). 3 more weeks to go. I will Pray for more understanding.

September 26, 1999. Here I am again. I missed a few days but I'm still blessed. God has been in Class with me. I was able to answere 1's that Boop and Gene Could not and that made my day. God is so Good. I Really fell off the wagon so to Speak. I went to the Dr on the 23rd. She Changed my Pressure RX and drew blood fo some more test. I go back in 1 month. I took Cory for his Ride on the bike today. I Needed that. Tomorrow is a New Day.

Ask God what He thinks of you every day from here on and for the rest of your life. That's the only opinion that matters.
—"The Heart of the Matter" audiotape

As the deer pants for streams of water, so my soul pants for you, O God.

Psalm 42:1

September 27, 1999

Today was not a bad day with food but I could have been better. I feel like I'm not in control like I was last week. Cory said to me when we were out Sunday with his bike that we needed to go all the way around because I need more exercise. I took him to McDonalds to get his ice cream Charles promised him and I bought a strawberry sundae for me. When he saw it he said "I don't think you are suppose to be eating that, I think you should ask Auntie if you can eat it." I missed my Monday night w/ Angela and Lynn. By the time the 4th Monday in Oct gets here I plan to have something to show.

September 28, 1999

Another day of eating Junk food that I should not have. I'm feeling like I need some exercise too after sitting all day. Tomorrow I will get on the scale and start over again.

September 29, 1999   2⁹⁸

Going in the wrong direction again. Today at work after almost completing the Training that started July 27, we find out that we will not be doing what we have been Trained on. We may even lose our Jobs. I will Pray on this I spoke with Angela about this. She said not to worry. Just take it to God in Prayer and let him handle it. She's so encouraging.

"I desire to do your will, O my God; your law is within my heart."

Psalm 40:8

October 2, 1999.
Today is a beautiful day. My funds Are short but I'm not staying in the house all day. Today I purchased A book by T.D. Jakes called "Lay Aside The Weight" and also "Prayer the Great Adventure by David Jeremiah. Tomorrow we go to see the Play "Lord Why do I Keep Choosing the wrong man"

October 3, 1999.
Cory and I went to the early service Rev Curry delivered the message. We came home and worked on Cory's school project. (Not Bad) Billy was suppose to pick-up Cory because I was going to see "Lord, why do I Always Chose the wrong man" (Billy was one of them) He didn't show or call so Angela decided to stay with Cory for me and Melissa went in her place. The show was Awsome. I throughly enjoyed that

blessing from Above. The Play will be
Coming back in Nov and I would
like to see it again. I'm sure of
one thing. The Lord will chose the next
Man in my life. I Certainly have made
Some bad Choices. But All of that is
behind me now. Well getting back to
my eating. I Need Control. I've Started
Veading "Lay Aside the Weigh"

October 4, 1999.
Not a bad day. Work was OK. I Passed
my Skill Check, Now 4 more days to go
And this Class will be over.

October 6, 1999.
I have been reading the Bibles every night
I have a Special Prayer each morning
when I get up and on the way to work
I talk with God. I'm feeling Changes. in
my life and I want to stay focused
on God And what his Plans Are for me.
I don't feel that He wants me to stay

He who tends a fig tree will eat its fruit, and he who looks after his master will be honored.

Proverbs 27:18

at Aetna. But I will continue to pray and wait on Him for the answer. Everything else is about the same. I saw Angela briefly today. Cory spent the day with Billy and that was good. God continues to bless me and I know it. I will continue to praise him.

October 10. 1999.

Cory and I went to 11:15 service. Its raining. The devil was trying to get me to stay home but I showed him. Shirley is not feeling well. She slept most of the day.

Shirley got worse. I called the ambul. and they took her to PG. She's not doing good.

October 26, 1994

Well So much has happen. Shirley is still in Critical Care @ PG She has improve A little She Smiles some but She has A Very long way to go. The Lord is keeping her safe and we Are all praying every day that he will soon delive her from this sickness and return he to us. I know that the Lord will provide for her. My job is another story. I don't think that I will be staying there. I will continue to pray on that the Lord will let me know how I should move on this.

He who conceals his sins does not prosper, but whoever
confesses and renounces them finds mercy.

Proverbs 28:13

October 16, 1999

I'm up @ 5:40 AM to take Angela and
Charles to BWI for their trip to Cancun.
Shirley is still in ICU. I pray to God
that He will let her come back to us
But I know that She is in his Care
and his Will shall prevail.

November 2, 1999

Well The Lord has prevailed. He has blessed
Shirley to come back to us. Yesterday she
was Talking & eating for the 1st time
since she has been in the hospital. She
is rapidly improving by the Grace of God
I thank you Lord for your Blessings
and I Praise your holy Name.
Went to See Shirley. She really has come
A long way. I'll be so glad when she is
back home and fully recovered.
I've Prayed on there & my situation.
I feel like she is taking Advantage of

Shirley being in the hospital. She had
her "girlfriend" upstairs yesterday. I know
that Clere has again said bad thing
about me to her but Romans 12:14
will be my guide.

November 3, 1999
What A beautiful Sunny cold day. I
Prayed that the Lord will bless us all
today. I Prayed for the world Problems
especially the People who feel Compelled to
take innocent People's lives like the
incident in Hawaii. The Lord is not Pleased.
The hospital called. They Put Shirley back
on the Ventalor last Night but they
will monitor her and maybe she can
come off of it today.

November 9, 1999   6:53 pm
Right Now I Just feel like Crying
and I Probley Will. I Wanted

*God will not hang your past over your head. He will never use
it against you. He is firm on you being obedient, but His
mercies are deep and wide and are "new every morning."*
—*"Dodging the Draft" audiotape*

First, I thank my God through Jesus Christ for all of you,
because your faith is being reported all over the world.

Romans 1:8

Wanted to See Shirley today but
I didn't have no one to watch Cory.
Shirley was moved from Critical Care
to a room today. Praise the Lord
for his goodness & Mercy.

November 21, 1999.
Shirley left PG Hospital last Wednesday and
She is now at Natl Rehab. Hosp. doing very good.
She is walking a little. We took her some
cloths also. God has brought her from a
mighty long way. It is possible that she
maybe home for "THANKSGIVING"
We all have a lOT to be Thankful For.

March 12, 2000.

Well a lot has happen since November 21st Shirley has recovered and on this coming Tuesday she will be having her Tonsils out. I pray to God that he will Continue to bless her in a mighty-way.

My Job is about the same. I've been on 1 interview at Southern MD Hospital. Ms. Walker said she was Quite pleased with our interview. I was not pleased with the Salary offered. So I'm still looking.

"Clare" Well let's see. She has been in PG Hospital from there to a drug treatment Center in Baltimore Back to Johnny's for 4 days and gone again. This time she Checked into Howard Univ Hospital. From there she went to stay with Cherita. Right now she is in Jail @ upper Marlboro. So many people are looking for her. It does not appear that she

---

Belief is much, much deeper than just something in your head. The information starts in your head, but then drops to your heart, and is then physically manifested in your actions.
—"Opposite World" audiotape

is trying to get any Help. Darryl's father was killed last Wednesday. There won't even be there for Darryle when he comes down to his fathers funeral. It does not seem to fase her 1 bit about the truma she has put Jenae d Darryle thru. I have turn her over to the Lord. His will Shall Prevail

_____

_____

_____

_____

_____

_____

_____

_____

_____

_____

_____

_____

_____

_____

_____

_____

_____

_____

_____

_____

_____

_____

The struggles in the desert are the pain and suffering from
obedience. *Desert pain is* not *the pain of disobedience.*
—"Backstroking the Red Sea," Desert Oasis '97

Brothers, I do not consider myself yet to have taken hold of it. But one thing I do: Forgetting what is behind and straining toward what is ahead . . . .

Philippians 3:13

_____

_____

_____

_____

_____

_____

_____

_____

_____

_____

_____

_____

_____

_____

_____

_____

_____

_____

_____

_____

_____

_____

_____

_____

If your will is to love God with all of your heart, your soul, and your mind, then you will hear His voice.
—"Stay Awake" audiotape

I have no greater joy than to hear that my children are walking in the truth.

III John 1:4

_Just open up your eyes, realize we are sons and daughters of the
richest, most powerful Being in the entire universe and He is
calling you._

—"The Heart of the Matter" audiotape

For great is his love toward us, and the faithfulness of the Lord
endures forever. Praise the Lord.

Psalm 117:2

_____

_____

_____

_____

_____

_____

_____

_____

_____

_____

_____

_____

_____

_____

_____

_____

_____

_____

_____

_____

_____

_____

_____

God . . . has shown us His passionate, jealous love, and He has shown us that He is not going to sit still and let the competition steal our hearts away.
            —"Backstroking the Red Sea," Desert Oasis '97

Blessed are they who keep his statutes and seek him with all their heart.

Psalm 119:2

_____

_____

_____

_____

_____

_____

_____

_____

_____

_____

_____

_____

_____

_____

_____

_____

_____

_____

_____

_____

_____

_____

_____

_____

_____

_____

_____

_____

_____

_____

_____

_____

_____

_____

_____

_____

_____

_____

_____

_____

_____

_____

_____

_____

_____

_____

God is very jealous of you giving your attention to food when
He rightfully deserves all that we have. . . .
　　　　　　　　　　　—"Emotional Eating" audiotape

By wisdom a house is built, and through understanding it is established; through knowledge its rooms are filled with rare and beautiful treasures.

Proverbs 24:3–4

_____

_____

_____

_____

_____

_____

_____

_____

_____

_____

_____

_____

_____

_____

_____

_____

_____

_____

_____

_____

_____

_____

_____

_____

_____

_____

_____

_____

_____

_____

_____

_____

_____

_____

_____

_____

_____

_____

_____

_____

_____

_____

_____

It is worth remembering that most real and lasting treasures in
life are slow in coming—but how wonderful it's going to be . . . .
—"The Prize and the Battle of the Will" audiotape

Blessed are the pure in heart, for they will see God.

Matthew 5:8

_____

_____

_____

_____

_____

_____

_____

_____

_____

_____

_____

_____

_____

_____

_____

_____

_____

_____

_____

_____

_____

_____

_____

_____

_____

_____

_____

_____

_____

_____

_____

_____

_____

_____

_____

_____

_____

_____

_____

_____

_____

_____

Be honest and truthful about where your heart is—whether it is still wanting to hold onto this earth or wanting to cling to the Father.

—"Backstroking the Red Sea," Desert Oasis '97

But seek first his kingdom and his righteousness, and all these things will be given to you as well.

Matthew 6:33

_____

_____

_____

_____

_____

_____

_____

_____

_____

_____

_____

_____

_____

_____

_____

_____

_____

_____

_____

_____

_____

_____

_____

_____

_____

_____

_____

_____

_____

_____

_____

_____

_____

_____

_____

_____

_____

_____

_____

_____

_____

_____

_____

_____

What happens if our heart is divided? If we love God and the food, too . . . it is simply impossible . . . . We cannot have two masters.

—"Backstroking the Red Sea," Desert Oasis '97

No one lights a lamp and hides it in a jar or puts it under a bed. Instead, he puts it on a stand, so that those who come in can see the light.

Luke 8:16

_____

_____

_____

_____

_____

_____

_____

_____

_____

_____

_____

_____

_____

_____

_____

_____

_____

_____

_____

*When you postpone your own control and relinquish decisions
to God, you are in essence believing in God's timing . . . and
you are proclaiming silently to the world that you believe God
is great!*

—"Hunger in the Desert," Desert Oasis '97

*For the bread of God is he who comes down from heaven and
gives life to the world.*

John 6:33

_____

_____

_____

_____

_____

_____

_____

_____

_____

_____

_____

_____

_____

_____

_____

_____

_____

_____

_____

_____

_____

There is an empty void in each of us that cannot be filled by earthly pursuits.

—"Jewels" audiotape

Therefore, since we have been justified through faith, we have peace with God through our Lord Jesus Christ . . . .

Romans 5:1

Christ is our sin offering, and there's a continual washing and regeneration of the heart every time you turn back to God and away from false gods.

—"Emotional Eating" audiotape

In him we have redemption through his blood, the forgiveness of sins, in accordance with the riches of God's grace that he lavished on us with all wisdom and understanding.
Ephesians 1:7–8

_____

_____

_____

_____

_____

_____

_____

_____

_____

_____

_____

_____

_____

_____

_____

_____

_____

_____

_____

_____

_____

_____

Jesus' sacrifice opened the door to the heart of God . . . . The
blood of Christ was used to part the Red Sea so that we could
simply walk across from Egypt to the arms of God on dry land.
—"Out of Egypt," Desert Oasis '97

"A little yeast works through the whole batch of dough."
Galatians 5:9

Once you get eating under control, God will surface something else, and then something else. It will bubble to the surface, and God will skim it off the top.

—"Opposite World" audiotape

Charm is deceptive, and beauty is fleeting; but a woman who fears the LORD is to be praised.

Proverbs 31:30

We must look deeper and relearn how to measure success in this life.

— "How to Measure Success" audiotape

The words of the wise are like goads, their collected sayings like firmly embedded nails—given by one Shepherd.

Ecclesiastes 12:11

_____

_____

_____

_____

_____

_____

_____

_____

_____

_____

_____

_____

_____

_____

_____

_____

_____

_____

_____

_____

You can't boast or brag of any wisdom you have. It is all a gift from the Giver.
          —"Above the Torture Zone" audiotape

*Do not let this Book of the Law depart from your mouth;
meditate on it day and night, so that you may be careful to do
everything written in it. Then you will be prosperous and
successful.*

Joshua 1:8

_____

_____

_____

_____

_____

_____

_____

_____

_____

_____

_____

_____

_____

_____

_____

_____

_____

_____

_____

_____

_____

_____

_____

_____

_____

_____

_____

_____

_____

_____

_____

_____

_____

_____

_____

_____

_____

_____

_____

_____

_____

_____

_____

_____

_____

_____

_____

_____

_____

*Our ways are not God's ways . . . . We are going to have to slow
down and find them.*

—"Opposite World" audiotape

Every good and perfect gift is from above, coming down from the Father of the heavenly lights, who does not change like shifting shadows.

James 1:17

_____

_____

_____

_____

_____

_____

_____

_____

_____

_____

_____

_____

_____

_____

_____

_____

_____

_____

_____

_____

_____

In the desert, you find that He can creatively accomplish anything you can imagine to pray for in Jesus' name.
—"Hunger in the Desert," Desert Oasis '97

Do not merely listen to the word, and so deceive yourselves. Do what it says.

James 1:22

_____

_____

_____

_____

_____

_____

_____

_____

_____

_____

_____

_____

_____

_____

_____

_____

_____

_____

_____

_____

_____

_____

_____

_____

_____

_____

_____

_____

_____

_____

_____

_____

_____

_____

_____

_____

_____

_____

_____

_____

_____

_____

You'll know it's a man-made rule because it will require no change from within . . . in your heart . . . . You'll know when it's a rule or command from God because it's going to require change.

—"Dodging the Draft" audiotape

No discipline seems pleasant at the time, but painful. Later on, however, it produces a harvest of righteousness and peace for those who have been trained by it.

Hebrews 12:11

_____

_____

_____

_____

_____

_____

_____

_____

_____

_____

_____

_____

_____

_____

_____

_____

_____

_____

_____

_____

*God is not going to give you more than you can bear . . . . You
will be in the eye of the hurricane and grounded in God so
deeply that you will always be able to sustain and will feel
peaceful.*

—"Emotional Eating" audiotape

Taste and see that the LORD is good; blessed is the man who takes refuge in him.

Psalm 34:8

_____

_____

_____

_____

_____

_____

_____

_____

_____

_____

_____

_____

_____

_____

_____

_____

_____

_____

_____

_____

_____

_____

_____

God has love to spare—overflowing, abundant rivers and seas of love.

— "The Promised Land," Desert Oasis '97

For, "Whoever would love life and see good days must keep his tongue from evil and his lips from deceitful speech."

I Peter 3:10

_____

_____

_____

_____

_____

_____

_____

_____

_____

_____

_____

_____

_____

_____

_____

_____

_____

_____

_____

_____

_____

_____

_____

_____

_____

_____

_____

_____

_____

_____

_____

_____

_____

_____

_____

_____

_____

_____

_____

_____

_____

_____

_____

Out of the abundance of the heart so the mouth speaks, and
what is in your heart will surface.
—"Hunger in the Desert," Desert Oasis '97

On my bed I remember you; I think of you through the watches of the night. Because you are my help, I sing in the shadow of your wings.

Psalm 63:6–7

_____

_____

_____

_____

_____

_____

_____

_____

_____

_____

_____

_____

_____

_____

_____

_____

_____

_____

_____

Open up your mouth and let Him fill up all your void feelings.
—"From Slavery to the Promised Land" audiotape

The angel of the LORD encamps around those who fear him, and he delivers them.

Psalm 34:7

_____

_____

_____

_____

_____

_____

_____

_____

_____

_____

_____

_____

_____

_____

_____

_____

_____

_____

_____

_____

_____

_____

_____

_____

_____

_____

_____

_____

_____

_____

_____

_____

_____

_____

_____

_____

_____

_____

_____

_____

_____

*Look at the fruit in your life from living these truths . . . . You
have just been delivered from the clutches of the mighty
Pharaoh, and you have been led across the Red Sea by the hand
of God.*

—The Weigh Down Diet

*Because of the L*ORD*'s great love we are not consumed, for his compassions never fail.*

Lamentations 3:22

_____

_____

_____

_____

_____

_____

_____

_____

_____

_____

_____

_____

_____

_____

_____

_____

_____

_____

_____

_____

_____

There is only one love that has a stronger magnetic pull than
the love of food—and it is the love of God.
                    —"Out of Egypt," Desert Oasis '97

*He answered: "'Love the Lord your God with all your heart and
with all your soul and with all your strength and with all your
mind'; and, 'Love your neighbor as yourself.'"*

Luke 10:27

_____

_____

_____

_____

_____

_____

_____

_____

_____

_____

_____

_____

_____

_____

_____

_____

_____

_____

_____

_____

_____

_____

_____

_____

_____

_____

_____

_____

_____

_____

_____

_____

_____

_____

_____

_____

_____

_____

_____

_____

_____

_____

_____

The key to permanent weight control lies . . . not in cutting the food in half, not in hunger and fullness, but the key to permanent weight loss lies in the heart of man.
—"Out of Egypt," Desert Oasis '97

Come near to God and he will come near to you.

James 4:8

_____

_____

_____

_____

_____

_____

_____

_____

_____

_____

_____

_____

_____

_____

_____

_____

_____

_____

_____

_____

_____

_____

_____

_____

_____

_____

_____

_____

_____

_____

_____

_____

_____

_____

_____

_____

_____

_____

_____

_____

_____

_____

_____

Our God is so good that even if our hearts have been misplaced,
we can—with a sincere, heartfelt focus—walk back again on
dry land to the sweet desert sand.
                    —"Backstroking the Red Sea," Desert Oasis '97

And now these three remain: faith, hope and love. But the greatest of these is love.

I Corinthians 13:13

It is easy *to serve the one you love . . . . You can't work your*
way to heaven—if you love *Him, you* will *obey Him.*
—"The Promised Land," Desert Oasis '97

So we say with confidence, "The Lord is my helper; I will not be afraid. What can man do to me?"

Hebrews 13:6

_____
_____
_____
_____
_____
_____
_____
_____
_____
_____
_____
_____
_____
_____
_____
_____
_____
_____
_____
_____
_____
_____
_____

_____

_____

_____

_____

_____

_____

_____

_____

_____

_____

_____

_____

_____

_____

_____

_____

_____

_____

_____

_____

_____

_____

*Control is all in the heart of a person and you do have a choice.
Do not be afraid.*

—The Weigh Down Diet

You, O Lord, reign forever; your throne endures from generation to generation.

Lamentations 5:19

_____

_____

_____

_____

_____

_____

_____

_____

_____

_____

_____

_____

_____

_____

_____

_____

_____

_____

_____

_____

_____

_____

He is a true God, because when you voluntarily give Him . . .
all of your heart, all of your soul, all of your mind, and all of
your strength . . . He gives it back to you one hundredfold.
Now, that's a true God.

—"Emotional Eating" audiotape

Therefore, since we are surrounded by such a great cloud of witnesses, let us throw off everything that hinders and the sin that so easily entangles, and let us run with perseverance the race marked out for us.

Hebrews 12:1

_____

_____

_____

_____

_____

_____

_____

_____

_____

_____

_____

_____

_____

_____

_____

_____

_____

_____

_____

_____

When you choose today whom you will serve and focus on,
your heart *will follow. It's automatic.*
—"Backstroking the Red Sea," Desert Oasis '97

Flowers appear on the earth; the season of singing has come,
the cooing of doves is heard in our land.

Song of Songs 2:12

God has so much passion for us. The evidence is everywhere around us. Open your eyes.

—"God's Passion for You" audiotape

"Blessed is the king who comes in the name of the Lord!"
"Peace in heaven and glory in the highest!"

Luke 19:38

He *is our Savior, for He has saved us from having to love the food, and we get to love Him.*
—"Out of Egypt," Desert Oasis '97

I have been crucified with Christ and I no longer live, but Christ lives in me. The life I live in the body, I live by faith in the Son of God, who loved me and gave himself for me.

Galatians 2:20

_____

_____

_____

_____

_____

_____

_____

_____

_____

_____

_____

_____

_____

_____

_____

_____

_____

_____

_____

_____

_____

_____

You need *to experience* need . . . . *In my darkest hour, God's*
approval was not only enough, it was more *than enough.*
—"Hunger in the Desert," Desert Oasis '97

The LORD will make you the head, not the tail. If you pay attention to the commands of the LORD your God that I give you this day and carefully follow them, you will always be at the top, never at the bottom.

Deuteronomy 28:13

_____

_____

_____

_____

_____

_____

_____

_____

_____

_____

_____

_____

_____

_____

_____

_____

_____

_____

_____

_____

_____

_____

_____

You can never outgive this Father we get to serve.
—"Jewels" audiotape

*The voice of the L*ORD *is powerful; the voice of the L*ORD *is majestic.*

Psalm 29:4

_____

_____

_____

_____

_____

_____

_____

_____

_____

_____

_____

_____

_____

_____

_____

_____

_____

_____

_____

_____

You will hear _the voice of the One you love._
—"The Promised Land," Desert Oasis '97

Dear friend, I pray that you may enjoy good health and that all may go well with you, even as your soul is getting along well.

III John 1:2

_____

_____

_____

_____

_____

_____

_____

_____

_____

_____

_____

_____

_____

_____

_____

_____

_____

_____

_____

_____

_____

_____

_____

_____

_____

_____

_____

_____

_____

_____

_____

_____

_____

_____

_____

_____

_____

_____

_____

_____

_____

_____

_____

_____

_____

_____

*Whenever you unplug yourself from God's line of authority,
you experience the threshold of confusion and the absence of
peace.*

—"The Promised Land," Desert Oasis '97

But godliness with contentment is great gain.

I Timothy 6:6

_____

_____

_____

_____

_____

_____

_____

_____

_____

_____

_____

_____

_____

_____

_____

_____

_____

_____

_____

_____

_____

_____

When we believe in God, we know about His desire to provide
for those devoted to Him.
     —"Hunger in the Desert," Desert Oasis '97

The thief comes only to steal and kill and destroy; I have come that they may have life, and have it to the full.

John 10:10

_____

_____

_____

_____

_____

_____

_____

_____

_____

_____

_____

_____

_____

_____

_____

_____

_____

_____

_____

_____

_____

_____

_____

_____

_____

_____

_____

_____

_____

_____

_____

_____

_____

_____

_____

_____

_____

_____

_____

_____

_____

_____

Do not let Satan ever rob you of your joy, because nothing can
come between you and this love for God when your heart cries,
"Abba, Father."

—"The Promised Land," Desert Oasis '97

For we fix our eyes not on what is seen, but on what is unseen.
For what is seen is temporary, but what is unseen is eternal.

II Corinthians 4:18

_____

_____

_____

_____

_____

_____

_____

_____

_____

_____

_____

_____

_____

_____

_____

_____

_____

_____

_____

_____

_____

*How can we ever know God if we have never released our
grasping hands, turning the palms up, waiting for Him to fill
them?*

—"Hunger in the Desert," Desert Oasis '97

The LORD is my strength and my song; he has become my salvation. He is my God, and I will praise him, my father's God, and I will exalt him.

Exodus 15:2

_____

_____

_____

_____

_____

_____

_____

_____

_____

_____

_____

_____

_____

_____

_____

_____

_____

_____

_____

_____

_____

*When you are throwing your heart toward the Father and
adoring Jesus, you will grow in confidence of God's love for
you.*

—"The Promised Land," Desert Oasis '97

And God blessed the seventh day and made it holy, because on it he rested from all the work of creating that he had done.

Genesis 2:3

_____

_____

_____

_____

_____

_____

_____

_____

_____

_____

_____

_____

_____

_____

_____

_____

_____

_____

_____

_____

_____

_____

_____

_____

_____

_____

_____

_____

_____

_____

_____

_____

_____

_____

_____

_____

_____

_____

_____

_____

_____

*This devotion belongs rightfully to the Creator of emotions—
God.*

—"Emotional Eating" audiotape

"This is the covenant I will make with them after that time, says the Lord. I will put my laws in their hearts, and I will write them on their minds."

Hebrews 10:16

We must set our minds on things above . . . . Those who wait in hope upon the Lord will soar on wings like eagles. Why? Because they are focusing upon the most important and leaving the less important behind.

—The Weigh Down Diet

*For, "All men are like grass, and all their glory is like the
flowers of the field; the grass withers and the flowers fall, but
the word of the Lord stands forever."*

I Peter 1:24–25a

_____

_____

_____

_____

_____

_____

_____

_____

_____

_____

_____

_____

_____

_____

_____

_____

_____

_____

_____

_____

_____

_____

_____

_____

_____

_____

_____

_____

_____

_____

_____

_____

_____

_____

_____

_____

_____

_____

_____

_____

*You can ignore the law of gravity and come to an early death.
In the same way, you can ignore this law of sin (the magnetic
pull to the love of worldly things) and come to an early
spiritual death.*

—"Rise Above" audiotape

God is our refuge and strength, an ever-present help in trouble.
Psalm 46:1

_____

_____

_____

_____

_____

_____

_____

_____

_____

_____

_____

_____

_____

_____

_____

_____

_____

_____

_____

_____

_____

_____

Humility means you are focused on Him and expect nothing from anyone except God.
—"Hunger in the Desert," Desert Oasis '97

Since, then, you have been raised with Christ, set your hearts on things above, where Christ is seated at the right hand of God. Set your minds on things above, not on earthly things.

Colossians 3:1–2

_____

_____

_____

_____

_____

_____

_____

_____

_____

_____

_____

_____

_____

_____

_____

_____

_____

_____

_____

_____

_____

_____

_____

Your job description is to love God and to stay focused on Him.
—"Hunger in the Desert," Desert Oasis '97

*"Who will not fear you, O Lord, and bring glory to your name?
For you alone are holy. All nations will come and worship
before you, for your righteous acts have been revealed."*

Revelation 15:4

_____

_____

_____

_____

_____

_____

_____

_____

_____

_____

_____

_____

_____

_____

_____

_____

_____

_____

_____

_____

_____

God wants it all. But when we make Him the master of our minds, we are free from the pull of food. Sounds good to me! Since we are going to be a slave to one or the other, I choose God!

—The Weigh Down Diet

*If you fully obey the L*ORD *your God and carefully follow all his commands I give you today, the L*ORD *your God will set you high above all the nations on earth.*

Deuteronomy 28:1

_____

_____

_____

_____

_____

_____

_____

_____

_____

_____

_____

_____

_____

_____

_____

_____

_____

_____

_____

_____

_____

_____

_____

_____

_____

_____

_____

_____

_____

_____

_____

_____

_____

_____

_____

_____

_____

_____

_____

_____

_____

_____

_____

_____

You have to fall back into God's arms and trust in Him, or you will fall back in fear.
—"Hunger in the Desert," Desert Oasis '97

Let love and faithfulness never leave you; bind them around your neck, write them on the tablet of your heart.

Proverbs 3:3

_____

_____

_____

_____

_____

_____

_____

_____

_____

_____

_____

_____

_____

_____

_____

_____

_____

_____

_____

_____

_____

_____

God's will is everything—life and peace and happiness.
—"Opposite World" audiotape

Choose my instruction instead of silver, knowledge rather than choice gold, for wisdom is more precious than rubies, and nothing you desire can compare with her.

Proverbs 8:10–11

When I gave Him my mind, He cleaned it up and made it pure, and He placed inside it more understanding than I had ever had before. He wants your mind, too. Give it to Him, for you will get much in return.

—The Weigh Down Diet

"'You have made known to me the paths of life; you will fill me with joy in your presence.'"

Acts 2:28

_____

_____

_____

_____

_____

_____

_____

_____

_____

_____

_____

_____

_____

_____

_____

_____

_____

_____

_____

_____

_____

_____

_____

_____

This is an extremely personal God. He puts the desires in your heart, and then He wants to fill them up.
—"Jewels" audiotape

Do not be anxious about anything, but in everything, by prayer and petition, with thanksgiving, present your requests to God.

Philippians 4:6

_____

_____

_____

_____

_____

_____

_____

_____

_____

_____

_____

_____

_____

_____

_____

_____

_____

_____

_____

_____

*When you believe in God, you know Him, and you know that
all you have to do is let Him know what you want and He will
take care of it.*
—"Hunger in the Desert," Desert Oasis '97

The Lᴏʀᴅ your God is with you, he is mighty to save. He will take great delight in you, he will quiet you with his love, he will rejoice over you with singing.

Zephaniah 3:17

_____

_____

_____

_____

_____

_____

_____

_____

_____

_____

_____

_____

_____

_____

_____

_____

_____

_____

_____

_____

_____

_____

_____

_____

_____

_____

_____

_____

_____

_____

_____

_____

_____

_____

_____

_____

_____

_____

_____

_____

_____

_____

_____

God is my *knight in shining armor, and God is* your *knight in shining armor. No one has ever—and no one* will *ever—fight for the right of your hand in a covenant relationship like God Almighty.*

—"Backstroking the Red Sea," Desert Oasis '97

*The Sovereign L*ORD *is my strength; he makes my feet like the feet of a deer, he enables me to go on the heights.*

Habakkuk 3:19

_____

_____

_____

_____

_____

_____

_____

_____

_____

_____

_____

_____

_____

_____

_____

_____

_____

_____

_____

_____

_____

_____

_____

_____

_____

_____

_____

_____

_____

_____

_____

_____

_____

_____

_____

_____

_____

_____

_____

_____

_____

_____

_____

_____

_____

_____

*This is one great God we serve, who has thought of absolutely
everything!*

—"Hunger in the Desert," Desert Oasis '97

*"The L*ORD *bless you and keep you; the L*ORD *make his face shine upon you and be gracious to you; the L*ORD *turn his face toward you and give you peace."*

Numbers 6:24–26

_____

_____

_____

_____

_____

_____

_____

_____

_____

_____

_____

_____

_____

_____

_____

_____

_____

_____

_____

_____

_____

_____